West Point Football IQ: The Ultimate Test of True Fandom

Gene Kraay

2011 Edition (Volume I)

Printed in the United States of America.
Copyright © 2011 by Gene Kraay.

All rights reserved. No part of this publication may be reproduced, stored in a retrieval system, or transmitted in any form or by any means, electronic, mechanical, recording, or otherwise, without the prior written permission of the author.

This title is part of the IQ sports trivia book series, which is a trademark of Black Mesa Publishing, LLC.

Cataloging-in-Publication Data is available from the Library of Congress.

ISBN: 978-0-9837922-8-4
First edition, first printing.

Cover photo courtesy of the United States Military Academy.

Black Mesa Publishing, LLC
Florida
David Horne and Marc CB Maxwell
Black.Mesa.Publishing@gmail.com

www.blackmesabooks.com

West Point Football IQ

To three fallen brothers-in-arms ...

Nick Hauck, USAFA Roommate and Thunderbird

Mike Blassie, Teammate and Warrior

Jim Egbert, Commander Extraordinaire

Contents

Introduction	1
First Quarter—Duty, Honor, Country	3
Second Quarter—The Team	15
Third Quarter—The Will To Win	27
Fourth Quarter—Leadership	39
Overtime—Morale	51
About the Author	63
References	64
About Black Mesa	65

"I want an officer for a secret and dangerous mission. I want a West Point football player."
— General of the Army George C. Marshall, Chief of Staff during World War II

Introduction

FEW FOOTBALL PROGRAMS – amateur or professional – boast the longevity or enjoy the rich tradition of the United States Military Academy at West Point.

Army football is as American as, well turkey and pumpkin pie on Thanksgiving Day. Beyond Heisman Trophy winners, All-Americans, Hall of Famers and National Champions, the West Point football program has produced leaders that have stood tall on battlefields around the world in defense of the values that make America great, players who have influenced and made history in venues far larger than a football stadium.

Army players touch a plaque before each home game inscribed with these words from General George C. Marshall, the Chief-of-Staff of the U.S. Army in World War II: "I want an officer for a secret and dangerous mission. I want a West Point football player." The plaque is there to remind these young athletes that there will indeed come a time for more important things than making a goal line stand or converting a fourth-and-long in the waning sunlight of a crisp, autumn afternoon on the banks of the Hudson River.

Perhaps this volume of questions will brighten the day of an old warrior who can recall a fond memory of his days in service when he stood shoulder to shoulder with his brothers-in-arms. Perhaps it will encourage some young and promising athlete to explore the opportunities at West Point.

Regardless, I hope every person who enters this book will find entertainment and value in the pages.

Gene Kraay
August 2011

"On the fields of friendly strife are sown the seeds that on other days and other fields will bear the fruits of victory."
— General of the Army Douglas MacArthur, West Point Graduate, National Football Foundation Gold Medal Winner

First Quarter—Duty, Honor, Country

AS AN ATHLETE, Douglas MacArthur played left field for the Army baseball team. MacArthur never played football as a cadet at West Point, but you will learn in this book that he was involved with the football team as well. Still, his influence on athletes at the United States Military Academy weighs powerfully through this quote that he delivered to the Cadet Corp: "On the fields of friendly strife are sown the seeds that on other days and other fields will bear the fruits of victory."

It is a message that is still taught at all of the service academies.

Established in 1802, West Point has always trained its cadets in accordance with the whole man concept: sound of heart, mind and body. Nothing less is expected of Army football players, and each knows that fitness in one of those elements, without fitness in the others will not be good enough 'on other days and other fields' when the stakes are significantly higher than a bowl bid.

As Superintendent of the United States Military Academy from 1919 to 1922, MacArthur was adamant that all members of the Cadet Corp participate in athletic competition throughout their years at the Academy, a requirement that remains to this day: every West Point cadet participates in varsity or intramural sports every day, and every cadet takes mandatory physical education classes throughout his or her four years at West Point. This at a time when physical education is no longer a mandatory part of even secondary school curriculum, much less college core curriculum.

The motto of the United States Military Academy is "Duty, Honor, Country," and MacArthur emphasized it over and over in his farewell speech to the Corp of Cadets on May 12, 1962: "Duty, Honor, Country: Those three hallowed words reverently dictate what you ought to be, what you can be, what you will be. They are your rallying points: to build courage when courage seems to fail; to regain faith when there seems to be little cause for faith; to create hope when hope becomes forlorn."

Every football player at West Point and all of their classmates lives and breathes those words.

QUESTION 1: The United States Military Academy – commonly referred to as West Point or Army – was established in 1802. In what year did Army play its first football game?
   a) 1870
   b) 1880
   c) 1890
   d) 1903

QUESTION 2: Army lost that first game. Who was Army's opponent?
   a) Navy
   b) Notre Dame
   c) Syracuse
   d) Michigan

QUESTION 3: What is West Point's mascot?
   a) The Black Knight
   b) The Ramblin' Wreck
   c) The Caisson
   d) The Mule

QUESTION 4: In what athletic conference does Army football play?
   a) The Patriot League
   b) The Big East
   c) America East
   d) Army plays as an Independent

QUESTION 5: What are Army football's traditional colors?
   a) Blue, Silver and Gold
   b) Gray, Black and Blue

c) White, Black and Silver
d) Black, Gold and Gray

QUESTION 6: What is the name of Army's football stadium?
a) Camp Randall Stadium
b) Michie Stadium
c) Veterans Memorial Stadium
d) Davis Wade Stadium

QUESTION 7: How many National Championships has Army won?
a) 0
b) 3
c) 8
d) 11

QUESTION 8: Which of these NFL coaches was an assistant coach at Army early in his career and later the head coach of Air Force for one season?
a) Dick Vermeil
b) Allie Sherman
c) Earl Blaik
d) Bill Parcells

QUESTION 9: In what year did Army win its last bowl game?
a) 2010
b) 1998
c) 1996
d) 2001

QUESTION 10: How many Heisman Trophy winners hail from West Point?
a) 0
b) 2
c) 3
d) 5

QUESTION 11: The United States Marine Corp team from Mare Island defeated Army in the 1918 Rose Bowl. Players from what base represented Army?
    a) Camp Savage, Minnesota
    b) Camp Williams, Utah
    c) Fort Campbell, Kentucky
    d) Camp Lewis, Washington

QUESTION 12: Sportswriters generally include one Army game in the 'short list' of "Games of the Century." Who was Army's opponent in that game in 1946?
    a) Syracuse
    b) Navy
    c) Ohio State
    d) Notre Dame

QUESTION 13: Army's "Game of the Century" ended in a tie. What was the final score?
    a) 0-0
    b) 6-6
    c) 9-9
    d) 14-14

QUESTION 14: The Lambert-Meadowlands Trophy has been awarded annually since 1936 to the best Division I team in the East. How many times has Army received the Lambert Trophy?
    a) 10
    b) 7
    c) 2
    d) Never

QUESTION 15: Not including the 1918 Rose Bowl when Army was represented by active duty soldiers, how many major bowl appearances has West Point made?
    a) 3
    b) 5

c) 6
d) 11

QUESTION 16: Who did Army defeat in the 1984 Cherry Bowl?
a) Tennessee
b) Kansas State
c) Michigan State
d) Missouri

QUESTION 17: Only one of these schools has more College Hall of Fame players than Army. Which one is it?
a) Notre Dame
b) Navy
c) Alabama
d) Nebraska

QUESTION 18: On November 13, 1920, Army recorded 13 rushing touchdowns against Bowdoin College in Maine, the most touchdowns West Point scored in a single game. What was the final score of the game?
a) 78-6
b) 90-0
c) 84-0
d) 83-14

QUESTION 19: What is the name of West Point's 'fan-fest' area located on the east side of the stadium on Mills Road?
a) Grant's Farm
b) Mule Train
c) Black Knights Alley
d) Hill and Dale

QUESTION 20: A St. Louis native is West Point's career rushing leader with 4,299 yards. Who is he?
a) Pete Dawkins
b) Mike Mayweather

c) Bobby Williams
  d) Larry Csonka

QUESTION 21: One of the most enduring football rivalries is the Army-Navy football game. How many times have the two academies played through the 2010 season?
  a) 57
  b) 71
  c) 111
  d) 121

QUESTION 22: In 1972, Army won the inaugural Commander-in-Chief's trophy, which is presented to the winner of the season series between Army, Navy and Air Force. How many times has West Point won the Commander-in-Chief's trophy?
  a) 15
  b) 6
  c) 17
  d) 12

QUESTION 23: These two West Point All-Americans played in the same backfield and were referred to as "Mr. Inside" and "Mr. Outside." Who is this tandem?
  a) Christian Cagle and "Red" Blaik
  b) Collin Mooney and Mike Mayweather
  c) Doc Blanchard and Glenn Davis
  d) Pete Dawkins and Bob Anderson

QUESTION 24: What was the last season in which Army was ranked nationally in the top 25?
  a) 2001
  b) 1996
  c) 1975
  d) Never

QUESTION 25: Which of these players was the first Army player to win the Heisman Trophy in 1945?

a) Joe Bellino
b) John David Crow
c) Les Horvath
d) Doc Blanchard

QUESTION 26: Since the inception of Army football over a century ago, 36 men have acted as head coach. Which one of these men was NOT a head coach at West Point?
a) Lou Saban
b) Tom Cahill
c) Rip Miller
d) Stan Brock

QUESTION 27: How many undefeated seasons has Army football enjoyed?
a) 4
b) 5
c) 6
d) 10

QUESTION 28: How many winless seasons has Army football endured?
a) 0
b) 1
c) 3
d) 6

QUESTION 29: Army's longest run from scrimmage was 97 yards, and it occurred in West Point's 48-7 win over Holy Cross in 1977. Who made that run?
a) Greg King
b) Jim Merriken
c) Jimmy Hill
d) Leamon Hall

QUESTION 30: This Army football player served two terms as President of the United States. Who was this player who once tackled Carlisle's Jim Thorpe?
  a) Gerald Ford
  b) Dwight Eisenhower
  c) Ronald Reagan
  d) Herbert Hoover

QUESTION 31: As a junior, this player was named to the All-America team as an end. The following season, he led Army to a 6-3 record at quarterback. Who was this player who graduated in 1956 with Norman Schwarzkopf?
  a) Tommy Bell
  b) Bob Anderson
  c) Don Holleder
  d) Pat Uebel

QUESTION 32: What Army football logo adopted in the '60s endured for three decades?
  a) The Bucking Bronco
  b) Ivanhoe
  c) The Kicking Mule
  d) The Holy Grail

QUESTION 33: Against what team did Army play on November 20, 2010, to mark the first football game to be played in the new Yankee Stadium?
  a) Navy
  b) Rutgers
  c) Air Force
  d) Notre Dame

QUESTION 34: What does the Corps of Cadets refer to its cheerleaders as?
  a) The Rabble Rousers
  b) Beetle Bailey's Battalion

c) Sgt. Rock's Easy Company
   d) The Gray Line

QUESTION 35: Who quarterbacked Army's first wishbone offense in 1984 and led his team to a national rushing title?
   a) Rob Healy
   b) Nate Sassaman
   c) Ricky Dobbs
   d) Troy Calhoun

QUESTION 36: What year did Army first play Air Force?
   a) 1959
   b) 1995
   c) 1957
   d) 1963

QUESTION 37: The Football Writers Association of America has awarded The Outland Trophy every year since 1946 to the best college football interior lineman. How many Army players have won the Outland Trophy?
   a) 6
   b) 3
   c) 1
   d) 0

QUESTION 38: Who did Army defeat 59-52 in double overtime on October 7, 1999, in West Point's first ever Thursday night home game?
   a) Louisville
   b) Boston College
   c) Syracuse
   d) Duke

QUESTION 39: Who did Army defeat in its first win ever by a score of 10-6?
   a) UConn Huskies
   b) Fordham Rams

c) Binghamton Bearcats
d) Princeton Tigers

QUESTION 40: In 1989, Army rushed for 631 yards – West Point's single game rushing record – against what team?
a) Appalachian State
b) BYU
c) Colgate
d) Delaware State

First Quarter Answer Key

___ **Question 1:** C
___ **Question 2:** A
___ **Question 3:** D
___ **Question 4:** D
___ **Question 5:** D
___ **Question 6:** B
___ **Question 7:** B
___ **Question 8:** D
___ **Question 9:** A
___ **Question 10:** C
___ **Question 11:** D
___ **Question 12:** D
___ **Question 13:** A
___ **Question 14:** B
___ **Question 15:** B
___ **Question 16:** C
___ **Question 17:** A
___ **Question 18:** B
___ **Question 19:** C
___ **Question 20:** B

___ **Question 21:** C
___ **Question 22:** B
___ **Question 23:** C
___ **Question 24:** B
___ **Question 25:** D
___ **Question 26:** C
___ **Question 27:** D
___ **Question 28:** C
___ **Question 29:** A
___ **Question 30:** B
___ **Question 31:** C
___ **Question 32:** C
___ **Question 33:** D
___ **Question 34:** A
___ **Question 35:** B
___ **Question 36:** A
___ **Question 37:** C
___ **Question 38:** A
___ **Question 39:** B
___ **Question 40:** C

Keep a running tally of your correct answers!

Number correct: ___ / 40

Overall correct: ___ / 40

"When you've got a bunch of guys wounded, you're not going anyplace, at least I'm not going anyplace, leaving wounded kids around — and that was the crux of the whole thing."
— Lieutenant General Bill Carpenter, Winner, Distinguished Service Cross

Second Quarter—The Team

WALTER CAMP DISTINGUISHED American Award winners understand the life-enduring lessons that football teaches, lessons like self-denial, cooperation and teamwork. In 1984, the Walter Camp Football Foundation presented this eminent award to former Army All-American Bill Carpenter.

Like the rest of his teammates, Carpenter graduated from West Point as a commissioned officer in the United States Army. He went on to serve multiple tours as an adviser and infantry officer in Vietnam.

On June 9, 1966, the lessons he learned in the '50s as a cadet and Army football player came into stark focus when he and his company were trapped on a ridgeline and under intense fire from an advancing North Vietnamese regiment that threatened to overrun their position and the battalion behind him commanded by Hank "The Gunfighter" Emerson, who graduated from West Point some ten years ahead of Carpenter.

As Emerson and other soldiers at the scene remembered the moments, Carpenter, ever cool under pressure, called in an airstrike on his own position.

"Bring it right on top of me. Put it on my smoke," Carpenter instructed the FAC (forward air controller) directing the supporting strike aircraft. He ignited a smoke grenade and tossed it 50 feet in front of him. The nearby battalion watched, stunned as air support rolled in and deployed napalm canisters into the jungle surrounding Carpenter and his company.[1]

By the end of the day, the battle was over. Miraculously, Carpenter's company, some 100 soldiers, sustained only eight casualties and none to napalm.

Recalls one member of Carpenter's company, "That napalm strike, I'm convinced, saved our lives." For his actions, Carpenter won the Distinguished Service Cross, the second highest military decoration.

---

[1] Sports Illustrated, October 4, 1993

Knute Rockne incited his players to "Win one for the Gipper." Schooled in decision-making on and off the field, Bill Carpenter needed direction and motivation from no one to make the play that would save hundreds of American lives on that chaotic battlefield in 1966.

QUESTION 41: What was the last year in which Army placed more than one player on a First Team, All-America football team?
 a) 1958
 b) 1923
 c) 1945
 d) 2001

QUESTION 42: Which Army player has the most 100-yard rushing games in a single season?
 a) Mike Mayweather
 b) Pete Dawkins
 c) Tommy Bell
 d) Tory Crawford

QUESTION 43: Which Army quarterback won the James E. Sullivan Award presented annually to the outstanding amateur athlete in the United States?
 a) Glenn Davis
 b) Frank Blanda
 c) Tom Lombardo
 d) Arnold Tucker

QUESTION 44: Army holds the NCAA Division I record in which category for a single season?
 a) Fewest yards allowed
 b) Most blocked punts
 c) Highest gain per rush
 d) Most rushes per game

QUESTION 45: On the last play of his collegiate career – in the 2008 Army-Navy game – this running back became Army's single season rushing leader. On that play, who eclipsed Mike Mayweather's previous mark by a single yard?
   a) Collin Mooney
   b) Edrian Oliver
   c) Rick Roper
   d) Demetrius Perry

QUESTION 46: What piece of football gear was arguably first worn at the 1893 Army-Navy football game?
   a) Shoulder pads
   b) Athletic supporter
   c) Cleated shoes
   d) Helmet

QUESTION 47: Which Army head coach is the only one to serve over ten seasons?
   a) Coach Earl H. Blaik
   b) Coach Bob Sutton
   c) Coach Stan Brock
   d) Coach Charles D. Daly

QUESTION 48: How many West Point head football coaches have there been through the 2010 season?
   a) 20
   b) 29
   c) 36
   d) 38

QUESTION 49: In what year did Bob Sutton win the Bobby Dodd National Coach of the Year award?
   a) 1989
   b) 1969
   c) 1998
   d) 1996

QUESTION 50: Which Army quarterback holds the single game passing yardage record?
   a) Zac Dahman
   b) Leamon Hall
   c) Carson Williams
   d) Tom Blanda

QUESTION 51: This Army football Hall of Famer flew 259 total combat missions, recorded 16 confirmed kills – 12 in WWII and four in Vietnam – and later served as the Commandant of Cadets at the United States Air Force Academy. Who is he?
   a) Chappie James
   b) Robin Olds
   c) Frank Merritt
   d) Karl Richter

QUESTION 52: In 2004, who eclipsed Glenn Davis's nearly 60-year old record for most rushing touchdowns in a single season?
   a) Michael Wallace
   b) Johnny Goff
   c) Josh Holden
   d) Carlton Jones

QUESTION 53: How many West Point graduates have been awarded the National Football Foundation Gold Medal?
   a) 2
   b) 4
   c) 6
   d) 8

QUESTION 54: Which of these cities has not hosted the Army-Navy game through the 2010 season?
   a) Pasadena, CA
   b) New York, NY
   c) Chicago, IL
   d) Washington, D.C.

QUESTION 55: Which Army lineman hustled nearly 70 yards and ran down seventh-ranked Duke's All-American Red Smith to make a miraculous, game-saving tackle late in the fourth quarter to preserve Army's 14-13 victory at the Polo Grounds in 1953?
 a) Bob Mischak
 b) Arnold Tucker
 c) Norman Schwarzkopf
 d) Ralph Chesnauskas

QUESTION 56: Which Army All-American led the team in rushing in both 1960 and 1961?
 a) John Seymour
 b) Al Rushatz
 c) Bob Anderson
 d) Sonny Stowers

QUESTION 57: This award honors the coach of Grambling State who holds the record for most Division I wins. Who is the only Army coach to win the Eddie Robinson Coach of the Year Award?
 a) Tom Cahill
 b) Jim Young
 c) Earl Blaik
 d) Bob Sutton

QUESTION 58: Which former Army coach played for the San Diego Chargers in Super Bowl XXIX?
 a) Bobby Ross
 b) Todd Berry
 c) Stan Humpries
 d) Stan Brock

QUESTION 59: In over 100 meetings, how many times has the Army-Navy game ended in a tie?
 a) 5
 b) 7

c) 11
  d) 14

QUESTION 60: Army's longest completed pass was 93 yards, and it occurred in West Point's 48-29 win over Cincinnati in 2004. Which Army quarterback threw the pass?
  a) Leamon Hall
  b) Joe Gerena
  c) Zac Dahman
  d) David Pevoto

QUESTION 61: Who did Army defeat in the 2010 Armed Forces Bowl in Fort Worth, Texas?
  a) TCU
  b) SMU
  c) LSU
  d) VMI

QUESTION 62: Which Army player who later went on to win the Bronze Star and Purple Heart in the Korean War won the Outland Trophy?
  a) Arnold Archibald, V
  b) Thomas Scott
  c) Joe Steffy
  d) John Minor

QUESTION 63: In memory of Don Holleder and the men of the 28th Infantry Regiment who died with him in Vietnam on October 17, 1967, the Army coaching staff presents this prestigious award. What is the name of this honored award?
  a) The Rolling Thunder Award
  b) The Black Lion Award
  c) The Black Watch Award
  d) The Red Badge of Courage Award

QUESTION 64: Which football Hall of Famer played tackle at West Point and later went on to serve as Director of Athletics at the United States Air Force Academy?
a) Hans Mueh
b) John Clune
c) Kevin Anderson
d) Frank Merritt

QUESTION 65: Army holds a winning record against which of these football programs?
a) Michigan
b) North Carolina
c) Syracuse
d) Pittsburgh

QUESTION 66: Midway through the 1909 schedule, Army cancelled the remainder of its season when Cadet Eugene A. Byrne died from injuries suffered against which team?
a) Duke
b) Harvard
c) Yale
d) Buffalo State

QUESTION 67: Since their first meeting in 1917, Army and Boston College have played 36 times. In what city did they play on November 19, 1988?
a) Boston, Massachusetts
b) Hartford, Connecticut
c) New York City
d) Dublin, Ireland

QUESTION 68: What is the name of the first Army mule, designated as "official" in 1936?
a) Pancho
b) Mr. Jackson
c) Spartacus
d) Hannibal

QUESTION 69: Which of these players was the second Army player to win the Heisman Trophy in 1946?
    a) Howard Cassaday
    b) Angelo Bertelli
    c) Glenn Davis
    d) John Cappelletti

QUESTION 70: Following the dedication game of Army's Michie Stadium, how many successive home games did West Point win?
    a) 3
    b) 9
    c) 40
    d) 53

QUESTION 71: Which Army Hall of Famer was known as the "Red Thunderbolt of West Point" and appeared on the cover of *Time Magazine*?
    a) Elmer Oliphant
    b) Doc Blanchard
    c) Joe Steffy
    d) Christian Cagle

QUESTION 72: Army's longest completed pass was 93 yards, and it occurred in West Point's 48-29 win over Cincinnati in 2004. Who received that pass?
    a) Tielor Robinson
    b) Aaron Alexander
    c) Walter Hill
    d) Jeremy Trimble

QUESTION 73: The year before Army set its NCAA Division I record for highest gain per rush, it set its other NCAA Division I record in which category for a single season?
    a) Fewest pass attempts per game average
    b) Fewest turnovers per game average

c) Most penalties per game average
   d) Most points scored per game average

QUESTION 74: Running back Al Rushatz was named a Kodak All-American in 1961. The previous year, he made the All-America team in what other sport?
   a) Boxing
   b) Wrestling
   c) Baseball
   d) Swimming

QUESTION 75: In what year did Army record its last tie score?
   a) 2005
   b) 1995
   c) 1993
   d) 1987

QUESTION 76: Where did Army play Air Force in their first meeting?
   a) Falcon Stadium, Colorado
   b) Michie Field
   c) Yankee Stadium
   d) Soldier Field, Chicago

QUESTION 77: Which West Point football season was cancelled after just one game due to armed conflict?
   a) 1918 due to WWI
   b) 1941 due to WWII
   c) 1951 due to the Korean War
   d) 1968 due to the Vietnam War

QUESTION 78: Who holds the Army record for most rushing yards in a single game?
   a) Mike Mayweather
   b) Michael Wallace
   c) Pete Dawkins
   d) Charlie Jarvis

QUESTION 79: Who rated West Point's Michie Stadium as one of the top 20 sports venues of the 20th century?
   a) Dick Vitale
   b) ESPN
   c) *Sporting News*
   d) *Sports Illustrated*

QUESTION 80: Which NCAA record did Army tie in its 1984 victory over Montana?
   a) Most players, same team, gaining 100 or more rushing yards in the same game
   b) Most 100 yard games by a quarterback
   c) Most first downs passing in a single game
   d) Most blocked punts in the same game

Second Quarter Answer Key

___ Question 41: A
___ Question 42: A
___ Question 43: D
___ Question 44: C
___ Question 45: A
___ Question 46: D
___ Question 47: A
___ Question 48: C
___ Question 49: D
___ Question 50: B
___ Question 51: B
___ Question 52: D
___ Question 53: C
___ Question 54: D
___ Question 55: A
___ Question 56: B
___ Question 57: A
___ Question 58: D
___ Question 59: B
___ Question 60: C
___ Question 61: B
___ Question 62: C
___ Question 63: B
___ Question 64: D
___ Question 65: A
___ Question 66: B
___ Question 67: D
___ Question 68: B
___ Question 69: C
___ Question 70: C
___ Question 71: D
___ Question 72: A
___ Question 73: D
___ Question 74: B
___ Question 75: B
___ Question 76: C
___ Question 77: A
___ Question 78: B
___ Question 79: D
___ Question 80: A

Keep a running tally of your correct answers!

Number correct: ___ / 40

Overall correct: ___ / 80

"Fighting spirit one must have. Even if a man lacks some of the other qualifications, he can often make up for it in fighting spirit."
— *Brigadier General Robin Olds, USAF, West Point Graduate, All-American*

Third Quarter—The Will To Win

NINETEEN-FORTY-TWO All-American lineman Robin Olds learned valuable lessons in leadership as an Army football player. As important as any of those lessons was the will to win, and his incessant drive to lead by example, to be the man at the tip of the spear.

While the years may cloud the truth from the legend ... as the story goes, in the 1942 Army-Navy game, Olds had his two, upper front teeth knocked out, which sidelined him for several plays while his mouth was stuffed with cotton to stop the bleeding. He returned to the game minutes later and knocked his former assailant flat on his back. As he stood smiling over his fallen opponent, he first pointed directly at his foe, then at his bleeding mouth. His return to the game and his bravado even drew cheers from the Navy sideline.

Twenty-four years later in 1966, the number of aerial losses sustained by Air Force F-105 Thunderchiefs to Soviet MIG aircraft over Southeast Asia became unacceptable. Of concern also was the lack of aggressiveness demonstrated by American pilots. Enter Col. Robin Olds as commander of the 8th Tactical Fighter Wing. Olds refused to sit on the sidelines and watch. He became a regular on the daily flight schedule and insured that he was treated no differently than the youngest pilot under his command.

Olds then proceeded to develop a strategy to draw the enemy MIGs to him and his F-4 Phantoms, which were better prepared for aerial combat that the Thunderchiefs, traditionally used to deliver ordinance to the ground. Olds' plan was code-named "Operation Bolo." On January 2, 1967, he put his plan to the test; he flew in the first flight at the tip of the spear. Olds scored the first win that day downing the enemy MIG with a heat-seeking Sidewinder missile. When the smoke cleared at the end of the day, Olds and his fellow pilots of the 8th TFW claimed seven kills.

Olds was undoubtedly a born leader, but his leadership skills and his commitment to lead by example were honed on the banks of the Hudson River where he led Army's hard-charging line on offense and defense for two varsity seasons in 1941 and 1942.

QUESTION 81: Which Army Mule presided over West Point's National Championship teams?
   a) Mr. Jackson
   b) Traveler
   c) Buckshot
   d) Ranger

QUESTION 82: In what year did Army last win the Commander-in-Chief's Trophy?
   a) 1979
   b) 1987
   c) 1996
   d) 2008

QUESTION 83: Which Army linebacker played his debut professional football game in 2010 with the Detroit Lions?
   a) Brian Zickefoose
   b) Cameron Craig
   c) Josh McNary
   d) Caleb Campbell

QUESTION 84: What media innovation first occurred at the 1963 Army-Navy game?
   a) The Goodyear blimp first appeared at a college football game
   b) The Golden Knights parachute team delivered the American flag to the stadium
   c) CBS introduced instant replay
   d) General Motors sponsored its first athletic contest

QUESTION 85: Which player on Army's undefeated 1958 team was dubbed "The Lonesome End" because he often lined up on the far sideline and did not huddle with the team?

a) Pete Dawkins
   b) Bill Carpenter
   c) Dan Foldberg
   d) Don Holleder

QUESTION 86: Which Army coach who refused to exempt his freshmen from the 13-mile Plebe hike during Beast Barracks said, "We're not going to win in spite of West Point. We're going to win because of West Point?"
   a) Bobby Ross, 2004-06
   b) Jim Young, 1983-90
   c) Earl Blaik, 1941-58
   d) Rich Ellerson, 2009-present

QUESTION 87: Army played 32 unbeaten games that began with the season opener against North Carolina in 1944. Who ended the unbeaten streak with a 21-20 upset on October 25, 1947?
   a) Columbia
   b) Notre Dame
   c) Navy
   d) USC

QUESTION 88: How did coach Paul Dietzel (1962-65) refer to his defensive specialist team?
   a) Howling Commandos
   b) The Wolfpack
   c) Chinese Bandits
   d) The Dirty Dozen

QUESTION 89: Who was the first West Point cadet to face Navy in three major sports: football, basketball and baseball?
   a) John G. Armstrong
   b) Robin Olds
   c) Earl H. Blaik
   d) Horatio B. Hackett

QUESTION 90: In 1944, West Point handed this fabled football program its worst defeat ever. Who did Army shut out 59-0 in that game?
   a) Michigan
   b) Notre Dame
   c) Texas
   d) Oklahoma

QUESTION 91: At the conclusion of the Army-Navy game, the alma mater of each team is played and sung. What do members of the winning team do while the alma mater of the losing team is played?
   a) They stand alongside the losing team and face the losing team's student body
   b) They do push-ups to equal the total score of the game
   c) They respectfully remove their helmets and take a knee
   d) They stand at attention and salute the losing team

QUESTION 92: Since what year has Army played Air Force every year?
   a) 1946
   b) 1959
   c) 1963
   d) 1971

QUESTION 93: Who holds Army's career interception record with 14?
   a) Glenn Davis
   b) Doug Pavek
   c) Pete Vann
   d) James Chun

QUESTION 94: Following graduation, Heisman winner Doc Blanchard flew fighter planes instead of playing professional football despite being the first-round draft pick of which NFL team?

a) Los Angeles Rams
b) Pittsburgh Steelers
c) Baltimore Colts
d) Chicago Bears

QUESTION 95: When asked if discipline was the key to winning, this two-time National Championship winning coach answered, "If it was, Army and Navy would be playing for the National Championship every year." Who is he?
a) Tom Osborne
b) Lou Holtz
c) Bo Schembechler
d) Bobby Bowden

QUESTION 96: In all but seven seasons, Army football has played as an "Independent." During those seven seasons, which conference did Army play in?
a) The Patriot League
b) The Big East
c) Conference USA
d) America East

QUESTION 97: Who was Army's first opponent from west of the Mississippi River?
a) St. Louis University
b) Kansas
c) Missouri
d) Texas A&M

QUESTION 98: What logo does Army display on its helmet?
a) Army has no logo on its helmet
b) A kicking mule
c) A medieval knight
d) Crossed sabers

QUESTION 99: In what informal athletic conference did Army participate prior to this conference's formal establishment in 1954?
a) The Ivy League
b) The Big Ten
c) The Big East
d) The ACC

QUESTION 100: What is Army's longest streak without a loss (includes two 0-0 ties)?
a) 23
b) 32
c) 18
d) 21

QUESTION 101: The last time an Army football player won the Heisman Trophy was in 1958. Who is he?
a) Alan Ameche
b) Doc Blanchard
c) Glenn Davis
d) Pete Dawkins

QUESTION 102: Only one school has received the Lambert Trophy more times than Army has. Who is it?
a) Penn State
b) Notre Dame
c) Boston College
d) Harvard

QUESTION 103: Who defeated Army in the 1988 Sun Bowl in El Paso, Texas?
a) Alabama
b) BYU
c) California
d) Dartmouth

QUESTION 104: What is the nickname for the West Point football team?
  a) The Golden Eagles
  b) The Mule Train
  c) The Black Knights
  d) The Light Brigade

QUESTION 105: What was the last year in which the Army-Navy game was not played?
  a) 1917
  b) 1929
  c) 1942
  d) 1969

QUESTION 106: Which General of the U.S. Army once served as the West Point football manager?
  a) Norman Schwartzkopf
  b) George Patton
  c) Omar Bradley
  d) Douglas MacArthur

QUESTION 107: From 1984 through 1999, Army successfully employed a "wishbone" offense. During those 15 years, how many national rushing titles did West Point capture?
  a) 1
  b) 2
  c) 3
  d) 4

QUESTION 108: The first West Point football player to earn All-America honors shares his name with a great Greek philosopher. Who was this All-American center?
  a) Socrates Romeyn
  b) Edward "Plato" Farnsworth
  c) Thales "Tilly" Ames
  d) Cicero Jarvis

QUESTION 109: Which team did Army defeat in the 1984 Mirage Bowl in Tokyo, Japan?
 a) Montana
 b) Oregon
 c) Arizona
 d) Kansas State

QUESTION 110: How many times has West Point hosted the Army-Navy football game?
 a) 3
 b) 12
 c) 17
 d) 56

QUESTION 111: Who did Army defeat 22-6 in 1971 before its largest home crowd ever (42,765)?
 a) The Citadel
 b) Missouri
 c) Air Force
 d) Tennessee

QUESTION 112: Through more than 120 football seasons, how many times has Army won ten games or more in a single season?
 a) Never
 b) Once
 c) Three
 d) Five

QUESTION 113: What football play was popularized when Army suffered its only loss in the 1913 season against Knute Rockne and Notre Dame?
 a) The forward pass
 b) The reverse
 c) The Statue of Liberty
 d) The point after touchdown

QUESTION 114: What award is presented to the winner of the Army-Navy football game?
a) The "Bragging Rights" plaque
b) The David Glasgow Farragut Cup
c) The Commander-in-Chief Trophy
d) The Thompson Cup

QUESTION 115: When does the Army-Air Force game most often occur?
a) The second Saturday in September
b) The first Saturday in October
c) The first Saturday in November
d) Billy Mitchell Day

QUESTION 116: Against which of these universities does Army hold a perfect win record?
a) Pennsylvania
b) New Hampshire
c) UConn
d) Vermont

QUESTION 117: In 1912, Army posted six wins against just two losses, one, a 0-6 loss against Navy, the other a 6-27 loss against the Carlisle Indian School. Who coached Carlisle against Army in that game?
a) Knute Rockne
b) Shorty Longman
c) Glenn Scobey "Pop" Warner
d) Doug Howard

QUESTION 118: Which Army player holds the single season reception record with 64?
a) Mike Fahnestock (1980)
b) Aaron Alexander (2003)
c) Bob Carpenter (1959)
d) Joe Albano (1970)

QUESTION 119: How long was Ian Hughes' record-setting punt against Air Force in November 1995?
 a) 88 yards
 b) 72 yards
 c) 71 yards
 d) 68 yards

QUESTION 120: Which team holds the record for most net yards gained against Army?
 a) UCLA
 b) Hawaii
 c) Miami
 d) Arkansas

Third Quarter Answer Key

___ QUESTION 81: A
___ QUESTION 82: C
___ QUESTION 83: D
___ QUESTION 84: C
___ QUESTION 85: B
___ QUESTION 86: D
___ QUESTION 87: A
___ QUESTION 88: C
___ QUESTION 89: C
___ QUESTION 90: B
___ QUESTION 91: A
___ QUESTION 92: D
___ QUESTION 93: A
___ QUESTION 94: B
___ QUESTION 95: D
___ QUESTION 96: C
___ QUESTION 97: B
___ QUESTION 98: A
___ QUESTION 99: A
___ QUESTION 100: B
___ QUESTION 101: D
___ QUESTION 102: A
___ QUESTION 103: A
___ QUESTION 104: C
___ QUESTION 105: B
___ QUESTION 106: D
___ QUESTION 107: D
___ QUESTION 108: C
___ QUESTION 109: A
___ QUESTION 110: A
___ QUESTION 111: B
___ QUESTION 112: B
___ QUESTION 113: A
___ QUESTION 114: D
___ QUESTION 115: C
___ QUESTION 116: D
___ QUESTION 117: C
___ QUESTION 118: B
___ QUESTION 119: A
___ QUESTION 120: B

Keep a running tally of your correct answers!

Number correct: ___ / 40

Overall correct: ___ / 120

"Leadership is intangible, and therefore no weapon ever designed can replace it."
— General Omar N. Bradley, West Point Graduate, Chairman of the Joint Chiefs of Staff

Fourth Quarter—Leadership

YOUNG OMAR BRADLEY excelled as a student while still captaining both the football and baseball teams at Moberly High School in small-town, central Missouri. Although he was known best at West Point for his power-hitting prowess and strong outfield arm on the baseball diamond, Bradley lettered in football in 1914.

Bradley and his teammate Dwight Eisenhower graduated in 1915 as members of the "Class the Stars Fell Upon" as it is commonly referred to at West Point. Bradley and Eisenhower were among 61 of the 164 graduates that year who went on to achieve the rank of General. Nine of those 61 future generals earned a varsity "A" on the football field.

Bradley had a keen eye for physical fitness, and when he took command of the 82nd Infantry Division two months after Pearl Harbor, he was greatly concerned over the physical condition of the new troops. Working with former 82nd soldiers like Medal of Honor winner Sergeant Alvin York, Bradley complemented the already tough, military training with an even more rigorous physical fitness program. The results would pay long-term dividends for the Allied war effort in WWII.

In 1943, Bradley reunited with his former teammate Dwight Eisenhower. Bradley orchestrated the final battles of the North African campaign, which resulted in the surrender of some 40,000 German soldiers.

In 1978, three years prior to his death, Omar Bradley received the Spirit of Independence Award at the Independence Bowl, first played two years earlier, and so named because it began in the bicentennial year. The award now bears Bradley's name. Each year, the Omar N. Bradley Spirit of Independence Award is presented to an American organization or citizen whose actions symbolize the spirit of freedom and independence on which the United States of America was founded.

Army football can be proud that so many of its alumni carry forward the lessons and the ideals that have enabled them to make positive contributions to their country for so long and in so many important and diverse ways.

QUESTION 121: Which All-American running back from Army did the Philadelphia Eagles select in the 1955 NFL draft?
 a) Pat Uebel
 b) Andy Peterson
 c) Bob Kyasky
 d) Tommy Bell

QUESTION 122: How did ESPN's analyst Shaun King refer to Army's 2008 offense?
 a) The Brock Bone
 b) The Chicken Wing
 c) The Ham Bone
 d) The Crazy Bone

QUESTION 123: The undefeated 1949 Army team was known for its physical play. During that season, Army shut out Navy 38-0 and recorded its second shutout against the Fordham Rams 35-0. How did the media refer to the contest in which Fordham captain Herb Seidell lost a tooth?
 a) The Battle of Bull Run
 b) Little Big Horn
 c) The Donnybrook on the Hudson
 d) The Greatest Show on Earth

QUESTION 124: Of the 34 states represented on West Point's 2010 fall roster, which state had the most players?
 a) Texas
 b) Pennsylvania
 c) Florida
 d) California

QUESTION 125: Which Army player was named the Associated Press's Male Athlete of the Year in 1946?
 a) Doc Blanchard
 b) Glenn Davis
 c) Pete Dawkins
 d) Joe Steffy

QUESTION 126: Army's 29-7 win over VMI in 2010 marked the 15th time the two military schools have met since 1917. Of the 15 games, how many has Army won?
 a) 3
 b) 8
 c) 10
 d) 14

QUESTION 127: What are the most consecutive games Army has played without being shut out?
 a) 28
 b) 39
 c) 82
 d) 93

QUESTION 128: Which of these opponents has never beaten Army?
 a) Stanford
 b) Wake Forest
 c) Michigan State
 d) Cornell

QUESTION 129: How many yards did Army put up against Alabama's defense – ranked fifth nationally – in the 1988 Sun Bowl?
 a) 350
 b) 413
 c) 134
 d) 53

QUESTION 130: Which Army quarterback ran for over 100 yards including a 22-yard touchdown in Army's 31-29 win over Illinois in the 1985 Peach Bowl?
a) Tory Crawford
b) Nate Sassaman
c) Rob Healy
d) Bryan McWilliams

QUESTION 131: Who was Army's first opponent at Michie Stadium?
a) Rutgers
b) Saint Louis University
c) Ball State
d) Temple

QUESTION 132: In how many decades has Army posted a winning percentage equal to or greater than .750?
a) 1
b) 2
c) 3
d) 4

QUESTION 133: During its 8-2, 1928 season, Army played two games at Yankee Stadium, the first against Notre Dame. Three weeks later, who did they play their second game against?
a) Stanford
b) SMU
c) Nebraska
d) Navy

QUESTION 134: In Army's 1984 Cherry Bowl win, the cadets tied the NCAA record for fewest pass attempts in a bowl game. How many passes did Army attempt in that game?
a) 0
b) 2
c) 3
d) 5

QUESTION 135: Which Army player won the 1985 Peach Bowl Defensive MVP Award?
   a) Jim Gentile
   b) Dave Scheyer
   c) Darius "Peel" Chronister
   d) Jim Jennings

QUESTION 136: How many First Team All-Americans has Army produced including players who were selected for more than one year?
   a) 6
   b) 27
   c) 71
   d) 41

QUESTION 137: Which Army player was awarded a Rhodes Scholarship and won an NCAA Postgraduate Scholarship in 1995?
   a) William Conner
   b) Michael McElrath
   c) Michael Thorson
   d) Eric Oliver

QUESTION 138: Since the inception of the Commander-in-Chief's Trophy in 1972, what is the largest victory margin Army has over Navy?
   a) 28
   b) 20
   c) 17
   d) 14

QUESTION 139: Which U.S. President called a special cabinet meeting to discuss the Army-Navy game, in which the superintendent of West Point recommended to the Secretary of War that the game be cancelled in the future?
   a) Grover Cleveland
   b) William McKinley

c) Theodore Roosevelt
d) Franklin Roosevelt

QUESTION 140: What is the approximate seating capacity of the West Point's Michie Stadium?
  a) 55,000
  b) 50,000
  c) 40,000
  d) 35,000

QUESTION 141: What is the name of the West Point band that entertains home crowds at halftime?
  a) The Hellcats
  b) Gabriel's Buglers
  c) Alexander's Rag Time Band
  d) Johnny Puleo's Harmonicats

QUESTION 142: This NFL great and three-time All-American at Syracuse University termed West Point's endurance test, "... the most grueling physical test I ever took." Who is he?
  a) Ernie Davis
  b) Jim Brown
  c) Larry Csonka
  d) Floyd Little

QUESTION 143: Notre Dame coach Ed McKeever was talking about an Army player when he said, "I have just seen Superman in the flesh. He wears number 35 ..." Who was he talking about?
  a) Glenn Davis
  b) Doc Blanchard
  c) Rudolph Cosentino
  d) Elwyn Rowan

QUESTION 144: What is the name of the award established in 1988 and reinstated in 2007 by Coach Stan Brock that acknowledges exceptional, near perfect play?

a) The Black Mamba Award
b) The Black Death Award
c) The Black Knight Award
d) The Black Hole Award

QUESTION 145: With the score tied 0-0 at halftime, Notre Dame coach Knute Rockne gave his "win one for the Gipper" speech to the Irish who went on to defeat Army 12-6. Where was that game held?
a) Blaik Field
b) Soldier Field
c) Yankee Stadium
d) Veterans Stadium

QUESTION 146: Now played in December, the first nearly 100 Army-Navy games were traditionally played the Saturday after which American holiday?
a) Halloween
b) New Years Day
c) Thanksgiving
d) Christmas Day

QUESTION 147: How many winless seasons – not including its inaugural, "single-game season" – has Army endured in over a century of football?
a) 1
b) 2
c) 4
d) 6

QUESTION 148: Who was Army's youngest football coach at 29-years old?
a) Harry Nelly
b) William Wood
c) Hugh Mitchell
d) Garrison "Gar" Davidson

QUESTION 149: How many yards per carry did Army average in 1945 when West Point set the NCAA Division I record for most rushing yards per carry average in a single season?
   a) 7.6
   b) 8.4
   c) 7.0
   d) 8.3

QUESTION 150: In what year was the first game played in Michie Stadium?
   a) 1908
   b) 1924
   c) 1934
   d) 1956

QUESTION 151: What team is Army's second oldest active rivalry?
   a) Rutgers
   b) Notre Dame
   c) Navy
   d) Virginia

QUESTION 152: What position did Pete Dawkins play?
   a) Halfback
   b) Quarterback
   c) Cornerback
   d) Center

QUESTION 153: During the three seasons he coached Army to the National Championship, this coach compiled 27 wins against zero losses and a single tie. Who was he?
   a) Vince Lombardi
   b) Tom Cahill
   c) Earl Blaik
   d) Paul Dietzel

QUESTION 154: What Big 10 team did Army defeat in the 1985 Peach Bowl?
   a) Michigan
   b) Illinois
   c) Missouri
   d) Indiana

QUESTION 155: The 1929 team captain, Christian Cagle played three seasons with which NFL franchise?
   a) Philadelphia Eagles
   b) New York Giants
   c) Baltimore Colts
   d) Washington Redskins

QUESTION 156: What popular spectator activity was introduced to Japan at the 1984 Mirage Bowl when Army defeated Montana 45-31?
   a) The Peanut Gallery
   b) Concession stands
   c) The Wave
   d) The Purple Haze

QUESTION 157: In 2008, Caleb Campbell was the first Army player to be drafted by the NFL since quarterback Ronnie McAda was selected by which NFL team in the 1997 draft?
   a) New York Giants
   b) Philadelphia Eagles
   c) New York Jets
   d) Green Bay Packers

QUESTION 158: The original construction cost of Michie Stadium is estimated at $300,000. In 2008, the state-of-the-art Hoffman Press Box was installed. How much did USMA '69 graduate Mark B. Hoffman pledge toward the construction cost of the press box?
   a) Less than $500,000
   b) Between $500,000 and $1 million

    c) $1 million to $3 million
    d) More than $3 million

QUESTION 159: How did quarterback Joe Caldwell pass signals to Bill Carpenter, "The Lonesome End" who stood near the far sideline outside of the huddles?
    a) With footwork
    b) With hand signals
    c) With Morse code
    d) Coach Blaik used a sideline runner

QUESTION 160: Which West Point cadet staged the kidnapping of Navy's goat prior to the 1953 Army-Navy game?
    a) Alexander Haig
    b) Buzz Aldrin
    c) Benjamin Franklin Schemmer
    d) Michael Collins

FOURTH QUARTER ANSWER KEY

___ **QUESTION 121**: D
___ **QUESTION 122**: A
___ **QUESTION 123**: C
___ **QUESTION 124**: A
___ **QUESTION 125**: B
___ **QUESTION 126**: D
___ **QUESTION 127**: D
___ **QUESTION 128**: C
___ **QUESTION 129**: A
___ **QUESTION 130**: C
___ **QUESTION 131**: B
___ **QUESTION 132**: D
___ **QUESTION 133**: A
___ **QUESTION 134**: B
___ **QUESTION 135**: C
___ **QUESTION 136**: C
___ **QUESTION 137**: D
___ **QUESTION 138**: B
___ **QUESTION 139**: A
___ **QUESTION 140**: C

___ **QUESTION 141**: A
___ **QUESTION 142**: D
___ **QUESTION 143**: B
___ **QUESTION 144**: B
___ **QUESTION 145**: C
___ **QUESTION 146**: C
___ **QUESTION 147**: B
___ **QUESTION 148**: D
___ **QUESTION 149**: A
___ **QUESTION 150**: B
___ **QUESTION 151**: A
___ **QUESTION 152**: A
___ **QUESTION 153**: C
___ **QUESTION 154**: B
___ **QUESTION 155**: B
___ **QUESTION 156**: C
___ **QUESTION 157**: D
___ **QUESTION 158**: D
___ **QUESTION 159**: A
___ **QUESTION 160**: C

KEEP A RUNNING TALLY OF YOUR CORRECT ANSWERS!

Number correct: ___ / 40

Overall correct: ___ / 160

"The best morale exists when you never hear the word mentioned. When you hear a lot of talk about it, it's usually lousy."
— General of the Army Dwight D. Eisenhower, West Point Graduate, President of the United States

Overtime—Morale

IN 1912, DWIGHT EISENHOWER won his letter "A" as a two-way player for the Army football team, a running back on offense and a linebacker on defense. That same season, however, he went down hard after a tackle and had to be carried off the field, sustaining a knee injury that ended his playing career at West Point.

Eisenhower was far from the common man who might have hung his head low and sought the sympathy of his teammates and classmates. Ever committed to his team and his school, Eisenhower became the head yell leader where he directed his energies no less passionately than he did as a player on the football field. His enthusiasm did not go unnoticed, and he was asked to coach the junior varsity football team, an assignment he accepted with pride.

Eisenhower rose to the rank of General of the Army and as Supreme Commander of the Allied Expeditionary Force in WWII, he was responsible for planning and executing the invasion of Europe in 1944. Through his nearly three decades of service following graduation in 1915 from West Point, Eisenhower was well known for his ability to lead and to motivate his troops. In one speech, Eisenhower proudly exhorted his troops with these words, "Together with millions of others of America's best, you have risen to defiantly shout 'It Shall Be Done,' and now you are offering your lives to prove your words ... as you go forth to take part in this greatest war ... may this flag sustain you."

Perhaps his greatest morale-building message was his Order of the Day, 6 June 1944:

"Soldiers, Sailors and Airmen of the Allied Expeditionary Force!

"You are about to embark upon the Great Crusade, toward which we have striven these many months. The eyes of the world are upon you. The hopes and prayers of liberty-loving people everywhere march with you. In company with our brave Allies and brothers-in-arms on other Fronts, you will bring about the destruction of the German war machine, the elimination of Nazi tyranny over the oppressed peoples of Europe, and security for ourselves in a free world.

"Your task will not be an easy one. Your enemy is well trained, well equipped and battle hardened. He will fight savagely.

"But this is the year 1944! Much has happened since the Nazi triumphs of 1940-41. The United Nations have inflicted upon the Germans great defeats, in open battle, man-to-man. Our air offensive has seriously reduced their strength in the air and their capacity to wage war on the ground. Our Home Fronts have given us an overwhelming superiority in weapons and munitions of war, and placed at our disposal great reserves of trained fighting men. The tide has turned! The free men of the world are marching together to Victory! I have full confidence in your courage and devotion to duty and skill in battle. We will accept nothing less than full Victory! Good luck! And let us beseech the blessing of Almighty God upon this great and noble undertaking."

Clearly, the lessons of leadership Eisenhower had learned on the football "Plain" at West Point had come to fruition.

QUESTION 161: What was the name of the film in which Doc Blanchard and Glenn Davis starred as themselves?
    a) *To Hell and Back*
    b) *The Spirit of West Point*
    c) *Boys Town*
    d) *The Long Grey Line*

QUESTION 162: In what year did Army first play a team from west of the Mississippi River?
    a) 1922
    b) 1934
    c) 1938
    d) 1964

QUESTION 163: What was West Point's first bowl appearance?
a) 1985 Cherry Bowl
b) 1984 Cherry Bowl
c) 1977 Lemon Bowl
d) 1985 Peach Bowl

QUESTION 164: How many complete seasons did Army play without suffering a loss at Michie Stadium?
a) 2
b) 3
c) 5
d) 7

QUESTION 165: Among the more than 80 coaches who have taken two different teams to bowl games is Army's Jim Young. What other team did Coach Young guide to three consecutive bowl victories?
a) Houston
b) Minnesota
c) Purdue
d) Mississippi

QUESTION 166: In which bowl game did all three Army Heisman Trophy winners compete?
a) The Sugar Bowl
b) The Bluebonnet Bowl
c) The Cotton Bowl
d) None ever played in a bowl game

QUESTION 167: Which Army football player was also the West Point boxing champ and is recognized by the NCAA as the 15th winningest football coach of all time (by percentage)?
a) Bob Neyland
b) Dennis Michie
c) Bob Stoops
d) Henry Williams

QUESTION 168: Who was the last consensus All-American from Army?
 a) Bob Anderson, 1957
 b) Brandon Rooney, 1999
 c) Bill Carpenter, 1959
 d) Mike Mayweather, 1990

QUESTION 169: Which Army line trio joined Doc Blanchard and Glenn Davis on the 1945 Associated Press First Team All-American Team?
 a) Casimir Myslinski, Joe Henry and Hank Foldberg
 b) Tex Coulter, Albert Nemetz and John Green
 c) Joe Steffy, Joe Stanowicz and John Foldberg, end
 d) Bud Sprague, Frank Merritt and Ed Garbish

QUESTION 170: Who was Army's MVP in West Point's 16-14 win over SMU in the 2010 Armed Forces Bowl?
 a) Quarterback Trent Steelman
 b) Linebacker Steve Erzinger
 c) Wide Receiver Davyd Brooks
 d) Linebacker Stephen Anderson

QUESTION 171: Through which years did Army's longest, consecutive streak without being shutout occur?
 a) 1983-91
 b) 1992-2000
 c) 1940-48
 d) 1927-32

QUESTION 172: Which Army linebacker won The Black Death Award for his exceptional play in Army's 14-7 win over Louisiana Tech in 2008?
 a) Josh McNary
 b) Frank Scappaticci
 c) Cameron Craig
 d) Mario Hill

QUESTION 173: In what years did Army's longest streak without a loss occur?
   a) 1944-47
   b) 1948-50
   c) 1957-59
   d) 1988-90

QUESTION 174: Which Army player won the 2011 Pat Tillman Award and finished his career as Army's all-time leader in sacks and tackles for loss?
   a) Andrew Rodriguez
   b) Stephen Anderson
   c) Josh McNary
   d) Marcus Hilton

QUESTION 175: How many undefeated home seasons has Army recorded in Michie Stadium?
   a) 0
   b) 7
   c) 14
   d) 31

QUESTION 176: What position did Doc Blanchard play?
   a) Halfback
   b) Quarterback
   c) Cornerback
   d) Fullback

QUESTION 177: What is the title of West Point's fight song?
   a) "The Caisson Song"
   b) "On Brave Old Army Team"
   c) "Over There"
   d) "God Bless America"

QUESTION 178: In 1990, how many 100-yard rushing games did Mike Mayweather have, the most ever in a single season by an Army player?

a) 8
b) 7
c) 5
d) 9

QUESTION 179: How many seasons did Vince Lombardi serve as an assistant coach under West Point legend Earl "Red" Blaik?
 a) 7
 b) 5
 c) 3
 d) 1

QUESTION 180: Which team did Army tie in its most recent stalemate in 1995?
 a) Rice
 b) Air Force
 c) Lehigh
 d) East Carolina

QUESTION 181: Which Army football player died in 1931 from injuries he received in West Point's 6-6 tie against Yale?
 a) John Price
 b) Biff Jones
 c) Richard Sheridan
 d) John McEwan

QUESTION 182: What is the name of the stadium annex located off the South end zone at Michie Stadium?
 a) Thayer Hall
 b) Herbert Center
 c) Kimsey Athletic Center
 d) Arvin Gymnasium

QUESTION 183: When CBS introduced instant replay in its 1963 broadcast of the Army-Navy game, commentator Lindsey Nelson told viewers, "Ladies and gentlemen, Army did not

score again." Who threw Army's winning touchdown on the play that became the first instant replay?
- a) Cammy Lewis
- b) Steve Lindell
- c) Frank Blanda
- d) Rollie Stichweh

QUESTION 184: Since 1972, how many times have Army, Navy and Air Force shared the Commander-in-Chief's Trophy?
- a) 4
- b) 6
- c) Twice
- d) Never

QUESTION 185: In it's undefeated 1945 National Championship season, Army set its record for fewest net yards allowed in a single game. How many net yards did Army yield in its game against Villanova that year?
- a) 96
- b) 12
- c) 99
- d) 33

QUESTION 186: Which NFL team selected Army's multiple 100-yard game running back Charlie Jarvis in the 1969 NFL draft?
- a) San Diego Chargers
- b) St. Louis Cardinals
- c) New York Giants
- d) Green Bay Packers

QUESTION 187: What jersey number did Doc Blanchard wear?
- a) 29
- b) 31
- c) 41
- d) 35

QUESTION 188: Which two Army football players married movie actresses?
a) Glenn Davis and Doc Blanchard
b) Pete Dawkins and Doc Blanchard
c) Robin Olds and Glenn Davis
d) Doug Kenna and Barney Poole

QUESTION 189: Which Army player holds the record for most receiving yards in a single season?
a) Mike Fahnestock (1980)
b) Jeremy Trimble (2007)
c) Clennie Brundige (1977)
d) Gary Steele (1966)

QUESTION 190: When Army and Navy last played to a tie in 1981, what was the final score?
a) 0-0
b) 3-3
c) 14-14
d) 8-8

QUESTION 191: Which Army player returned as head football coach and then came back two decades later as a Major General to serve as the Superintendent of the United States Military Academy?
a) Ralph Sasse
b) Laurence Bliss
c) Harvey Jablonsky
d) Garrison "Gar" Davidson

QUESTION 192: After being named captain of the Army football team in 1959, he walked to Lusk Reservoir on the West Point campus and said, "They want me to follow in Pete Dawkin's footsteps. I have to learn how to walk on water." Who said these famous words?
a) Frank Gibson
b) Bill Carpenter

c) Ed Szvetecz
d) Al Vanderbush

QUESTION 193: In 1958, Army won its first homecoming game 35-6 against which opponent?
a) Virginia
b) West Virginia
c) Penn State
d) Villanova

QUESTION 194: How many points per game did Army's 1944 record setting team average?
a) 58
b) 61
c) 56
d) 49

QUESTION 195: Carlton Jones holds the single season record for rushing touchdowns with how many TDs?
a) 12
b) 15
c) 17
d) 21

QUESTION 196: Which Army quarterback directed West Point's wishbone attack to a school record ten wins in a single season and a fifth consecutive win over Navy?
a) Ronnie McAda
b) Zac Dahman
c) Johnny Goff
d) Rick Roper

QUESTION 197: In what year did Army's two-way lineman Joe Steffy win the Outland Trophy?
a) 1917
b) 1974

c) 1939
d) 1947

QUESTION 198: Army lost the 1996 Independence Bowl by a field goal. Who defeated them?
a) North Carolina
b) Auburn
c) Texas A & M
d) Air Force

QUESTION 199: What position did Glenn Davis play?
a) End
b) Quarterback
c) Halfback
d) Safety

QUESTION 200: According to the tradition introduced in 1901 by President Theodore Roosevelt, on which side of the field will the President of the United States sit when he attends the Army-Navy game?
a) With the team who won the previous year's contest
b) With the team who lost the previous year's contest
c) One half with Army and one half with Navy
d) Alternates from year to year

Overtime Answer Key

___ QUESTION 161: B   ___ QUESTION 181: C
___ QUESTION 162: A   ___ QUESTION 182: C
___ QUESTION 163: B   ___ QUESTION 183: D
___ QUESTION 164: D   ___ QUESTION 184: A
___ QUESTION 165: C   ___ QUESTION 185: B
___ QUESTION 166: D   ___ QUESTION 186: A
___ QUESTION 167: A   ___ QUESTION 187: D
___ QUESTION 168: C   ___ QUESTION 188: C
___ QUESTION 169: B   ___ QUESTION 189: A
___ QUESTION 170: D   ___ QUESTION 190: B
___ QUESTION 171: A   ___ QUESTION 191: D
___ QUESTION 172: B   ___ QUESTION 192: B
___ QUESTION 173: A   ___ QUESTION 193: A
___ QUESTION 174: C   ___ QUESTION 194: C
___ QUESTION 175: D   ___ QUESTION 195: C
___ QUESTION 176: D   ___ QUESTION 196: A
___ QUESTION 177: B   ___ QUESTION 197: D
___ QUESTION 178: A   ___ QUESTION 198: B
___ QUESTION 179: B   ___ QUESTION 199: C
___ QUESTION 180: A   ___ QUESTION 200: C

KEEP A RUNNING TALLY OF YOUR CORRECT ANSWERS!

Number correct: ___ / 40

Overall correct: ___ / 200

West Point Football IQ

It's time to find out your West Point Football IQ. Add your total from all five chapters and see how you did! Here's how we interpret your total score:

190-200 = 5-STAR BLACK KNIGHT IQ EXCEEDS ULYSSES S. GRANT

170-189 = 4-STAR BLACK KNIGHT IQ DESTINED TO BE A COMMANDING GENERAL

150-169 = 3-STAR BLACK KNIGHT IQ IS WORTHY OF A BCS TITLE

140-159 = 2-STAR BLACK KNIGHT IQ IS WORTHY OF ALL-AMERICAN STATUS

120-139 = GENERAL BLACK KNIGHT IQ ALLOWS YOU FULL RETIREMENT BENEFITS

100-119 = COLONEL BLACK KNIGHT IQ EARNS A LUNCH WITH THE PRESIDENT

80-99 = MAJOR BLACK KNIGHT IQ EARNS YOU A DESK AT THE PENTAGON

60-79 = CAPTAIN BLACK KNIGHT IQ LETS YOU CLEAN THE MAJOR'S DESK AT THE PENTAGON

40-59 = LIEUTENANT BLACK KNIGHT IQ LETS YOU FEED THE ARMY MULE

0-39 = YOU ARE AWOL (absent without leave), CLIMB BACK INTO YOUR FOXHOLE

About the Author

GENE KRAAY was an All-American Soccer Player in 1969 at the United States Air Force Academy in Colorado. He flew the single-seat, single-engine, Mach 2+ F-106 Delta Dart in the old Aerospace Defense Command. He spent nearly 45 years in military and corporate aviation. Writing as E.S. Kraay, he has three historical novels to his credit: *The Olympian, A Tale of Ancient Hellas; The Hamsa*; and *Tobit and the Hoodoo Man, A Mystical Tale from the Civil War South*. He has optioned the film rights to *The Olympian*. Gene and Marie, his wife of 38 years reside outside of Tucson in the Sonoran Desert. They have four grown children, three sons and one daughter, four grandchildren and three dogs. Their daughter Stefanie [Golan] is the Head Women's Soccer Coach at West Point. You can learn more about his novels at www.eskraay.com.

References

- GoArmy.com
- SportsLogo.com
- NCAA.org
- SportsIllustrated.com
- ESPN.com
- ArmyNavyGame.com
- Sports.Ap.org
- Woopido.com
- CBSSports.com

About Black Mesa

BLACK MESA IS a Florida-based publishing company that specializes in sports history and trivia books. Look for these popular titles in our trivia IQ series:

- *Mixed Martial Arts (Volumes I & II)*
- *Boston Red Sox (Volumes I & II)*
- *Tampa Bay Rays*
- *New York Yankees*
- *Atlanta Braves*
- *Milwaukee Brewers*
- *St.. Louis Cardinals (Volumes I & II)*
- *Major League Baseball*
- *Cincinnati Reds*
- *Texas Rangers*
- *Boston Celtics*
- *Florida Gators Football*
- *Georgia Bulldogs Football*
- *Texas Longhorns Football*
- *Oklahoma Sooners Football*
- *Texas A&M Aggies Football*
- *Buffalo Bills*
- *New England Patriots*

For information about special discounts for bulk purchases, please email:

black.mesa.publishing@gmail.com

www.blackmesabooks.com

Also in the Sports by the Numbers Series

- *Major League Baseball*
- *New York Yankees*
- *Boston Red Sox*
- *San Francisco Giants*
- *Texas Rangers*
- *University of Oklahoma Football*
- *University of Georgia Football*
- *Penn State University Football*
- *NASCAR*
- *Sacramento Kings*
- *Mixed Martial Arts*

The following is an excerpt from

Curse in the Rearview Mirror: Boston Red Sox IQ, Volume II

Bill Nowlin

Available from Black Mesa Publishing

First

There's the anticipation leading up to the game. Long gone are the days that it was easy to stroll up to the Fenway Park box office and put down your money to buy a ticket and then walk right in. It's still possible to get game of day tickets, every game, but you can't count on there being many and if you are two or more wanting to sit together, the difficulty increases. There's also the scalp-free zone where you can buy tickets at no more than list price, and very often less, just before the game. You can also decide to get scalped and maybe pay an arm and a leg, depending – of course – on the laws of supply and demand. And there are the ticket resellers like StubHub or Ace Tickets or the ones who had the great TV ad a couple of years ago, Hig's.

You get into the park – always a little bit of an extra rush even if you've been to hundreds of games – maybe watch some batting practice. Someone throws out the ceremonial first pitch, there's the National Anthem, and finally, the real first pitch.

First up are the visitors (it wasn't always that way in major-league history, but it's been that way for a long, long time). The home team gets to bat last.

You don't really want to be late. Real fans don't understand it when they're going with a friend, and he/she doesn't have the same urgency to get there. I liken it to going to a movie. Why would you want to come in 10 minutes into the film?

Imagine showing up in time for the top of the second inning on June 27, 2003. You would have missed seeing the Red Sox score 14 runs in the bottom of the first inning off the Marlines. The game was pretty much over before it began and the crowd was buzzing all game long ... but you would have missed it.

Imagine what you would have missed if you'd missed the first two batters in the 1917 game on June 23. You would have missed seeing Babe Ruth punch umpire Brick Owens and get thrown out the game, and seeing Ernie Shore come in and start his perfect game.

On May 18, 2002, if you'd missed just the first nine pitches of the game, you would have missed seeing Pedro Martinez strike out the side, setting down Seattle with three strikeouts.

Every game starts with a first inning. And a lot can happen in the first.

TOP OF THE FIRST

QUESTION 1: What player hit a home run for the Red Sox, and then attended his college graduation that same day?

QUESTION 2: Which one of the following played against the Red Sox, rather than for them?
- a) Aristotle
- b) Archimedes
- c) Beckett
- d) Dante
- e) Darwin
- f) Emerson
- g) Ulysses
- h) Albert Schweitzer

QUESTION 3: What player never hit a grand slam throughout his entire Red Sox career until his final season, when he hit four of them?
- a) Mike Greenwell
- b) Ted Williams
- c) Jackie Jensen
- d) Babe Ruth
- e) Manny Ramirez

QUESTION 4: What new record did Jonathan Papelbon set in 2010?

QUESTION 5: Who hit the one-hopper that was famously "stabbed by Foulke"?

QUESTION 6: Four of the 10 American Leaguers to hit two grand slams in the same game were Red Sox players. Which one of the following was not one of the four?
   a) Nomar Garciaparra
   b) Ted Williams
   c) Rudy York
   d) Jim Tabor
   e) Bill Mueller

QUESTION 7: Can you recall who was the winning pitcher of what was arguably the greatest game in Red Sox history? We're talking Game Four of the 2004 ALCS against the Yankees.
   a) Curtis Leskanic
   b) Keith Foulke
   c) Curt Schilling
   d) Mike Timlin
   e) Pedro Martinez

QUESTION 8: Which Red Sox player made the most errors in one World Series game?

QUESTION 9: Errors happen more often than one might think. What is the longest stretch of games in which the Red Sox played error-free baseball?

QUESTION 10: How did the Church of the Redemption unintentionally prevent 50 Red Sox games from being played at Fenway Park?

Top of the First Answer Key

___ **Question 1:** Harry Agganis – and he didn't have far to go. It was June 6, 1954. Harry hit a two-run home in the fifth inning, for the fifth and sixth runs in a 7-4 win over the Tigers, then went down the street and graduated from Boston University after the game.

___ **Question 2:** If you guessed the guy with the first and last name, you're right. Schweitzer was a right fielder for the St. Louis Browns from 1908 to 1911, known by the nickname "Cheese". He figured in Smoky Joe Wood's July 29, 1911 no-hitter against the St. Louis Browns, batting third and going 0-for-3. The other names are reflected in the following Red Sox player names: Aristotle "Harry" Agganis, Arquimedez Pozo, Josh Beckett, Dante Bichette, Danny Darwin, Emerson Dickman, and Ulysses "Tony" Lupien. The Sox also fielded a Cicero, a coach named Euclides, a Godwin, and a couple of Bards.

___ **Question 3:** Answer: Babe Ruth

___ **Question 4:** His save of Beckett's 3-1 lead over the Indians on August 3 gave him 25 saves on the season, making him the first pitcher in major-league history to record 25 or more saves in each of his first five seasons in the big leagues.

___ **Question 5:** Cardinals shortstop Edgar Renteria, grounding out 1-3 to end the 2004 World Series.

___ **Question 6:** Answer: B – Ted Williams.

___ **Question 7:** Don't panic – it was Curtis Leskanic.

___ **Question 8:** In five chances, Bill Mueller made three errors in Game Two of the 2004 World Series, which the Red Sox won, 6-2, over the Cardinals. Mueller was 2-for-3 at the plate.

___ **QUESTION 9:** In 1987, the Red Sox played the first game of the season without committing an error. Adding this game to the final 10 games of the 1986 regular season, that was a stretch of 11 consecutive errorless games – longest in franchise history.

___ **QUESTION 10:** Because the park was less than 1,000 feet from Fenway Park, a local statute prohibited the Red Sox from playing at Fenway on Sundays. From April 28, 1929 through May 29, 1932, the team was 17-31 with two ties in games held at Braves Field.

KEEP A RUNNING TALLY OF YOUR CORRECT ANSWERS!

    Number correct: ___ / 10

    Overall correct: ___ / 10

BOTTOM OF THE FIRST

QUESTION 11: In terms of intentions, which Red Sox player once received four intentional walks in one game?

QUESTION 12: Which Red Sox player holds the American League record for most intentional walks in a season?

QUESTION 13: When Daisuke Matsuzaka singled in Game Three of the 2007 World Series, it was the first time a Red Sox pitcher had a hit in the World Series since ... who?

QUESTION 14: Roger Clemens pitched three no-hit innings to kick off the 1986 All-Star Game in Houston, and received the win. At the time, he was the only Red Sox pitcher to record an All-Star Game victory. Six had taken the loss: Lefty Grove, Tex Hughson, Frank Sullivan, Monbouquette, Radatz, Tiant, and Eckersley – which is a pretty good collection of pitchers. Can you name the three Red Sox pitchers who have won All-Star Games since Clemens?

QUESTION 15: What five-time 20-game winner was signed by the Red Sox, but only appeared in one game - and lost it?
    a) Matt Clement
    b) Tom Seaver
    c) Jim Palmer
    d) Tony Clark
    e) Jack Chesbro

QUESTION 16: Can you name an American League pitcher who once won 41 games in a season for New York but whose career Red Sox record was 0-1?
    a) Herb Pennock
    b) Red Ruffing
    c) Jack Chesbro
    d) Mike Torrez

QUESTION 17: Who was the last Red Sox player to wear #9 before Ted Williams?
   a) Gordie Hinkle
   b) Dusty Cooke
   c) Bobby Doerr
   d) Ben Chapman

QUESTION 18: Which uniform number has been worn by more different Red Sox players than any other number?

QUESTION 19: Name the Red Sox player who wore the highest number of anyone in team history.

QUESTION 20: What Red Sox player finished his playing career with the Washington Senators but later had his number retired by the Red Sox?

Bottom of the First Answer Key

___ **Question 11:** Manny Ramirez on June 5, 2001.

___ **Question 12:** Ted Williams, 33 (1957) – a record he shares with John Olerud (1993).

___ **Question 13:** Bill Lee, in Game Seven of the 1975 Series.

___ **Question 14:** Pedro Martinez – 1999; Josh Beckett – 2007; Jonathan Papelbon – 2009.

___ **Question 15:** E – Jack Chebsro.

___ **Question 16:** C – Chesbro was 41-12 in 1904 for New York, but 0-1 for the Red Sox in 1909.

___ **Question 17:** Chapman. The four men listed each wore #9 before Ted, in the order listed.

___ **Question 18:** #28 – worn by 58 different players or coaches in the years since 1931, when the Red Sox first wore numbers.

___ **Question 19:** J. T. Snow wore #84 in 2006.

___ **Question 20:** Johnny Pesky, who played for both the Tigers and then the Senators in 1954.

Keep a running tally of your correct answers!

Number correct: ___ / 10

Overall correct: ___ / 20

www.blackmesabooks.com

www.ingramcontent.com/pod-product-compliance
Lightning Source LLC
Chambersburg PA
CBHW061500040426
42450CB00008B/1432